Early Stages of Litigation Attorney Survey
Report to the Judicial Conference Advisory Committee on Civil Rules

Emery G. Lee III

Federal Judicial Center
March 2012

Contents

Executive Summary

At the request of the Judicial Conference Advisory Committee on Civil Rules, the Federal Judicial Center designed and conducted a closed-case survey about the early stages of litigation, especially Federal Rules of Civil Procedure 26(f) and 16(b). The survey was sent to almost 10,000 attorneys of record in civil cases terminated in July–September 2011 and yielded a 36% response rate.

Key findings of the survey include:

- 72% of all survey respondents reported that, in the sampled case, they met and conferred with the opposing side to plan for discovery, as required by Rule 26(f). Among respondents also reporting a Rule 16(b) scheduling conference with a judge in the sampled case, the comparable figure was 92%.

- The most common method of conducting the Rule 26(f) meeting was by telephone or videoconference, reported by 86% of respondents with a meeting.

- Most respondents with a Rule 26(f) meeting in person and/or by telephone reported that the meeting lasted between 10 and 30 minutes.

- 71% of respondents with a Rule 26(f) meeting reported that the meeting assisted them in making arrangements to make initial disclosures in the sampled case, 60% reported that it helped in developing a proportional discovery plan, 50% reported that it helped them to better understand the opposing side's claims and/or defenses, 40% reported that they discussed discovery of electronically stored information, and 30% reported that the meeting increased the likelihood of a prompt resolution of the sampled case.

- Of the 40% of respondents reporting a discussion of discovery of electronically stored information at the Rule 26(f) meeting, 60% reported discussing preservation obligations.

- 50% of all respondents, and 60% of respondents with a Rule 26(f) meeting, reported a Rule 16(b) scheduling conference, either in person or by telephone, with a judge in the sampled case.

- Most respondents with a Rule 16(b) conference in person or by telephone reported that the conference lasted between 10 and 30 minutes.

- 94% of respondents with a Rule 16(b) conference also reported a scheduling order in the sampled case.

- Attorneys representing plaintiffs at least half of the time were asked whether their pleading practices have changed since the *Twombly* and *Iqbal* decisions. Half said yes, half said no. The most common change in pleading practices reported was including more factual detail in complaints, reported by 92% of those with changed practices.

Background

At its November 2011 meeting, the Judicial Conference Advisory Committee on Civil Rules requested that the Federal Judicial Center (FJC) design and conduct a survey[1] about the early stages of litigation, focused on Federal Rules of Civil Procedure 26(f) and 16(b). The survey was designed with the assistance of members and staff of the advisory committee. Because some parts of the survey touched upon case events that might occur in a relatively small subset of cases, such as the discussion of preservation obligations related to electronically stored information, the decision was made to survey a rather large sample of attorneys. A 24% sample was drawn from 29,627 civil cases terminated in July–September 2011, after excluding several nature-of-suit codes[2] and cases that terminated in less than 90 days. From those 7,134 cases, emails for 12,334 attorneys were drawn from the courts' records. After de-duplication, this yielded almost 10,000 attorney emails—9,978, to be precise, almost equally divided between plaintiff and defendant attorneys in the sampled cases. An email inviting these attorneys to answer the survey was sent in mid-January 2012, with one reminder email in late January. The survey drew 3,552 responses, for a response rate of 36%.

Rule 26(f) Meetings

Incidence of Rule 26(f) Meetings

In what percentage of cases are parties meeting and conferring to plan for discovery, as required by Rule 26(f)? This is not as straightforward a question as it may at first appear. Many cases terminate in a relatively short time, for example, and thus will not endure long enough for a meeting of the parties for this purpose. (Throughout this report, I will use the term "meeting," although parties may complete their Rule 26(f) obligations without, in fact, ever meeting in person. I will clarify when in-person meetings are meant.) Other cases terminate by default judgment—it would be difficult to meet with a defendant who does not answer.

The survey asked, "After the filing of the complaint and before the first Rule 16(b) conference (sometimes called a scheduling or case management conference), did you or any attorney for your client confer with opposing counsel—by telephone, correspondence, or in person—to plan for discovery in the named case (hereinafter "the conference")?" As can be seen in Table 1,[3] fully 72% of respondents answered yes, 21% no, and 7% declined to answer. Considering just the first two responses, 78% of respondents reported a Rule 26(f) meeting and 22% reported that there was no such meeting.

---

1. My FJC colleagues Margaret Williams and George Cort provided invaluable assistance in conducting this research.

2. *See* Emery G. Lee III & Thomas E. Willging, Federal Judicial Center National, Case-Based Civil Rules Survey (Federal Judicial Center, October 2009) (hereinafter "Civil Rules Survey"), at 77, for a discussion of sampling methods. The sampled cases were drawn exclusively from original proceedings and removals from state court.

3. Tables are found in the Appendix.

It may be useful to compare this finding to other studies. Recently, the FJC survey of attorneys in recently closed complex cases in the Southern District of New York found that 59% of respondents reported a Rule 26(f) meeting; the comparable figure for respondents answering yes or no was 68%. The 2009 Civil Rules survey included the same question. In that survey, 83% of respondents indicated that a Rule 26(f) meeting had taken place in the sampled case.[4] The comparable figure for respondents answering yes or no was 86%. The 2009 results, however, are limited to respondents who also reported that some sort of discovery took place in the sampled case. That is probably the reason that the 2009 Civil Rules survey produces the highest percentage of respondents reporting a Rule 26(f) meeting of the three studies.

The lack of a Rule 26(f) meeting does not necessarily mean that the parties disregarded the rule. As can be seen in Table 1, Rule 26(f) meetings were reported by 92% of respondents who also reported a Rule 16(b) scheduling conference in the sampled case but by only 61% of respondents who reported that there was no Rule 16(b) scheduling conference. This suggests that the parties are planning for discovery in almost all cases that get as far as a Rule 16(b) scheduling conference.[5] Moreover, the survey followed up with respondents who indicated that no Rule 26(f) meeting had taken place in the sampled case (Table 2). The most common reason given (other than "other") was that the case had been resolved before a conference could be held, 30%. Another 12% of respondents indicated that the case was of a type exempted from Rule 26(f). Moreover, a large number of the other responses indicated that the case was not one in which a Rule 26(f) meeting would be likely to occur (e.g., remands, default judgments, review of an administrative record without discovery).

The survey included response options for the "why not" question that are, from a Rules-perspective, simply invalid. Relatively few respondents selected these options: 6% reported that the parties agreed to forgo the Rule 26(f) meeting in the sampled case, 5% that one side refused to meet, and 2% that, "As a general practice, I do not participate in those conferences." (That 2% comprised 17 attorneys.)

In sum, the available evidence suggests that Rule 26(f) meetings are being conducted in most civil cases—at least 70%—and that these meetings are being held in the vast majority of cases in which discovery takes place or a Rule 16(b) conference is held.

How Rule 26(f) Meetings Are Conducted

The most common form of meeting was by telephone or videoconference, reported by 86% of respondents with a Rule 26(f) meeting in the sampled case (Table 3). Conferring by correspondence, including email, was reported by 25% of respondents. Only 9% of respondents reported an in-person meeting as part of the

---

4. Civil Rules Survey, *supra* note 2, at 7.

5. An FJC study found that the average time from case filing to entry of the first docketed scheduling order was 4.1 months. *See* Emery G. Lee III, The Timing of Scheduling Orders and Discovery Cut-Offs (Federal Judicial Center, October 2011), at 2.

Rule 26(f) process. (And obviously, respondents could indicate multiple forms of meeting.)

Respondents reporting a telephonic and/or in-person meeting were asked to estimate how long, in total, the meeting(s) took. As can be seen in Table 4, the most common response was 10–30 minutes, reported by 54% of all respondents. Fully 73% of all respondents reporting a Rule 26(f) meeting by telephone and/or in-person reported that the meeting took 30 minutes or less.

Given the generally short amount of time reportedly spent in most Rule 26(f) meetings, it is not surprising that 74% of respondents reported that they were able to complete the meeting in a single conversation. Fully 96% of respondents reported that they had sufficient time to adequately plan for discovery prior to the Rule 16(b) conference.

The survey also asked, "Prior to the conference, did you receive any instruction from the court—beyond what is found in the national rules—on how to conduct the conference?" Fully 34% of respondents answered affirmatively. Of those respondents, 44% reported that the instructions were in the form of a local rule and/or standing order; 33%, an order in the case; 32%, the individual practices of the presiding judge; 6%, other communication from the court; and 2%, other (Table 5).

Attorney Evaluations of the Rule 26(f) Meeting

Respondents reporting a Rule 26(f) meeting in the sampled case were asked a series of questions to evaluate the helpfulness of the meeting:

- Did the meeting help you to understand better the opposing side's claims and/or defenses in the case?
- Did the meeting increase the chances of a prompt settlement or resolution of the case?
- Did the meeting help in making arrangements for initial disclosures in the case?
- Did the conference include discussion of electronically stored information?
- In retrospect, did the meeting help to develop a plan that kept the volume of discovery in the case proportional to the stakes?

Table 6 summarizes the responses to these questions (these are percentages for those answering yes or no only). The Rule 26(f) meeting was rated as most helpful in making arrangements for initial disclosures, with 71% of respondents reporting a Rule 26(f) meeting answering yes, and 60% reported that the meeting helped to develop a proportional discovery plan. Half of respondents reported the meeting helped them to better understand the opposing side's claims and/or defenses. Only 30% reported that the meeting increased the chances of a prompt settlement or resolution. (The 40% of respondents who reported a discussion of electronically stored information will be discussed in the next section.)

The survey followed up with both yes and no responses. Those answering yes were asked to rate, on a 5-point scale, from 1, very little, to 5, a great deal, how helpful the meeting was in achieving the goal specified in the prompt. For all four questions, the average rating was between 3.1 and 3.4—i.e., respondents tended to rate the meeting as helpful, but not greatly so.

For no answers, the survey provided respondents with a list of reasons why the conference might not have been helpful. The most common response, for each goal, was as follows:

- "I generally understood the opposing side's claims and defenses prior to the conference," 77% of no answers;
- "At least one party was not interested in settlement or resolution at this point," 60%;
- "The initial disclosure obligation was clear prior to conference," 58%;
- "Other" was the most common response to the proportionality question, 33%.[6]

Interestingly, lack of cooperation from opposing counsel was offered as an option for the no responses, but few respondents indicated that uncooperative counsel was the reason that the Rule 26(f) meeting was not useful. (For a complete breakdown, see Tables 7–10.)

Overall, 60% of all respondents, and 74% of respondents reporting a Rule 26(f) meeting in the sampled case, reported submitting a discovery plan to the court.

Electronic Discovery

As mentioned in the previous section, only 40% of respondents reported discussing discovery of electronically stored information as part of the Rule 26(f) meeting.[7] The survey then asked those respondents whether that discussion included discussion of any party's preservation obligations with respect to that information. Of those who discussed electronically stored information, 60% reported discussing preservation obligations. Overall, that means that just 25% of all respondents discussed electronic discovery issues at a Rule 26(f) meeting, and only 13% of all respondents discussed preservation obligations.[8]

Those who discussed preservation obligations were then asked how helpful that discussion was in defining their client's (asked of producing parties) or the opposing side's (requesting parties) preservation obligations. Fully 60% of producing parties and 74% of requesting parties reported that the discussion clarified preservation obligations (Table 11). The most common response as to why the

---

6. It is worth noting that many respondents had difficulty answering this particular question—fully 1 in 4 respondents reporting a Rule 26(f) meeting were unable to answer the "In retrospect" question yes or no.

7. For the sake of comparison, the FJC survey of attorneys in recently closed complex cases in the Southern District of New York found that no electronic discovery was planned in 46% of respondents' cases. The 2009 Civil Rules Survey found that about 1 in 3 respondents reported discussing electronically stored information at the Rule 26(f) meeting. *See* Civil Rules Survey, *supra* note 2, at 15.

8. Just to be clear, these percentages are of all survey respondents, regardless of whether they reported a Rule 26(f) meeting at all. These percentages must be taken into account in the design of future studies. If preservation is discussed in about one closed case for every 8 (13%), then any study of such discussions must begin with a relatively large sample size—unless, that is, some means to identify those cases in advance can be devised.

discussion did *not* provide clarification was that the preservation obligations were clear before the conference—89% of producing parties and 79% of requesting parties who said that the Rule 26(f) meeting did not help to clarify preservation obligations gave this as the reason (Tables 12–13).

As with the questions discussed in the previous section, respondents who indicated that the Rule 26(f) meeting helped to define preservation obligations were asked to rate on a 5-point scale its helpfulness in doing so. Again, respondents tended, on average, to give middling answers—3.1 for producing parties, 3.2 for requesting parties.

Rule 16(b) Conferences

Incidence of Rule 16(b) Conferences

Overall, 50% of all respondents reported that, in the sampled case, there was no Rule 16(b) conference, 31% reported an in-person meeting with a district or magistrate judge, and 19% reported a telephonic Rule 16(b) conference (percentages of respondents answering yes or no, excluding "Can't say" responses) (Table 14). Among respondents reporting a Rule 26(f) meeting in the sampled case, 39% reported that there was no Rule 16(b), 38% reported an in-person meeting with a district or magistrate judge, and 22% reported a telephonic Rule 16(b) conference.

Respondents answering that there was no Rule 16(b) conference were asked a follow-up question: "Why wasn't there a Rule 16(b) conference in person or by telephone?" The most common response was that the case was resolved before holding a conference, reported by 40% (Table 15). Another 24% of respondents reported that the case was not required to have a Rule 16(b) conference under a local rule or judicial order, and 12% of respondents indicated that the Rule 16(b) conference was conducted by correspondence. For 24% of respondents, the reason given for the lack of a Rule 16(b) conference was "other."

Overall, 55% of the Rule 16(b) conferences in the sampled cases were held in person, 34% by telephone, and 11% on the papers.

How Rule 16(b) Conferences Are Conducted

The survey identified 1,587 respondents reporting that a Rule 16(b) conference was held, either in person or by telephone, in a sampled case. These respondents overwhelmingly reported that lead counsel for both sides participated in the Rule 16(b) conference—84%, compared to 14% reporting lead counsel for one side only, and just 1%, reporting no lead counsel participation (Table 16). Respondents were split fairly evenly between those reporting that the conference was conducted by a district judge, 50%, or a magistrate judge, 47%, with an additional 3% (42 attorneys) reporting "other" (Table 17). These responses were sometimes "both," but included respondents reporting that a judge's law clerk, courtroom deputy, or secretary conducted the Rule 16(b) conference.

Respondents were asked whether the judge engaged in a substantive discussion of the sampled case at the Rule 16(b) conference (Table 18). Fully 63% of respondents with a Rule 16(b) conference answered yes, and 37% answered no. The next question asked how long the Rule 16(b) conference lasted (Table 19). As with Rule 26(f) meetings, Rule 16(b) conferences tended to be 30 minutes or less in length. Indeed, 23% of respondents with a Rule 16(b) conference reported that the conference lasted less than 10 minutes. Most respondents, 57%, reported that the conference lasted between 10 and 30 minutes. Together, that means that 80% of the reported Rule 16(b) conferences lasted less than 30 minutes. An additional 17% of respondents reported a Rule 16(b) conference of 30 minutes to an hour, and 3% reported a conference of more than an hour in length.

The two previous questions can be analyzed together—respondents were more likely to report that the judge was substantively engaged in a conference that lasted more than 10 minutes (Table 20). Of those with a conference of less than 10 minutes, only 31% reported that the judge engaged with the substance of the case. That figure jumps to 69% of those reporting a conference of 10 to 30 minutes, 82% of those reporting a conference of 30 minutes to an hour, and 89% of those reporting a conference of more than an hour.

Respondents were asked whether the judge engaged in a discussion of the proportionality of discovery requests relative to the stakes and whether the judge limited discovery to make it more proportional in the sampled case. Just 24% and 16% of respondents, respectively, reported that the judge did so (Tables 21–22).

Scheduling Orders

Fully 94% of respondents with a Rule 16(b) conference reported that the judge entered a scheduling order after the conference (Table 23). The survey asked respondents whether the court set cut-off dates for fact discovery, reported by 79%, expert discovery, 70%, dispositive motions, 69%, amended pleadings, 65%, and joinder of additional parties, 59% (Table 24). Only 11% of respondents answered that the judge did not impose cut-offs for discovery in the sampled case.

Respondents were asked whether the judge adopted the parties' proposed discovery plan without modification, with minor modification, or with major modification (Table 25). The most common response was with minor modification, 57%, followed by without modification, 39%, and with major modification, 4%.

Respondents were also asked how often the scheduling order in the sampled case was modified (Table 26). The most common response was that the order was modified occasionally, reported by 50%, followed by the order was not modified but the case settled before deadlines were reached, 30%, the order was not modified and deadlines were enforced, 15%, and the order was modified frequently, 6%.

Respondents were asked to rate, on a 5-point scale, from 1, not all involved, to 5, very actively involved, how involved the presiding judge was in the management of the sampled case. Among all respondents, the average response was 2.6. Among respondents reporting a Rule 16(b) conference, the average response was 2.9. Among respondents reporting that the judge engaged in a substantive discussion of the case at the Rule 16(b) conference, the average response was 3.1.

Twombly/Iqbal **Questions**

Given the advisory committee's continued interest in the impact of *Twombly* and *Iqbal*, the survey asked attorneys primarily representing plaintiffs or representing plaintiffs and defendants about equally whether their pleading practices had changed since the Supreme Court's decisions in those cases (Table 27). Interestingly, half of respondents (answering yes or no) reported their pleading practices had changed, and half reported that they had not.

A follow-up question was asked of those reporting a change in pleading practices—specifically, how had their pleading practices changed as a result of the decisions? The most common answer, by far, was that plaintiff attorneys reported including more factual detail in complaints, reported by 92% of those with changed pleading practices (Table 28).

Appendix: Descriptive Tables

Table 1: After the filing of the complaint and before the first Rule 16(b) conference (sometimes called the scheduling or case management conference), did you or any attorney for your client confer with opposing counsel—by telephone, correspondence, or in-person—to plan for discovery in the named case?

Category of Respondent	Yes (%)	No (%)	Can't say (%)	N
2012 ESOL Survey				
All respondents	72	21	7	3,538
Respondents answering "yes" or "no"	78	22	-	3,284
Respondents answering "yes" or "no" with Rule 16(b) conference	92	8	-	1,478
Respondents answering "yes" or "no" without Rule 16(b) conference	61	39	-	1,513
SDNY Complex Survey				
All respondents	59	29	13	312
Respondents answering "yes" or "no"	68	32	-	274
2009 Civil Rules Survey				
Respondents with discovery	83	13	4	2,371
Respondents with discovery answering "yes" or "no"	86	14	-	2,276

Table 2: Why didn't you or an attorney for your client confer with opposing counsel to plan for discovery in the named case? (Select all that apply.)

2012 ESOL Survey Response	(%)
The case was resolved before the conference could take place	30
Scheduling difficulties	4
The parties agreed to forego the conference	6
One side refused to meet and confer	5
The conference was not required by the court (e.g., exception under Rule 26(a)(1)(B))	12
As a general practice I do not participate in these conferences	2
Other	45
N	734

Table 3: How was the Rule 26(f) meeting conducted? (Select all that apply.)

2012 ESOL Survey Response	(%)
In-person meeting	9
By telephone or videoconference	86
By correspondence, including via email	25
N	2,550

Table 4: If held in person or by telephone or videoconference, how long was the conference? If the conference was not completed in one session, please estimate the total time taken up by all the sessions?

2012 ESOL Survey Response	(%)
Less than 10 minutes	19
10–30 minutes	54
30 minutes–1 hour	20
More than 1 hour	8
N	2,326

Table 5: If respondent indicated that, prior to the Rule 26(f) meeting, s/he received instructions from the court on how to conduct the meeting, what form did those instructions take? (Select all that apply.)

2012 ESOL Survey Response	(%)
Local rule	44
Standing order	44
Individual practices of presiding judge	32
Order in particular case	33
Other communication from court	6
Other	2
N	861

Table 6: Attorney evaluations of Rule 26(f) meeting, percentage of respondents answering "yes," excluding non-responses.

2012 ESOL Survey Response	Yes (%)	*N*
Help you better understand the opposing side's claims and/or defenses?	50	2,287
Increase the chances of a prompt settlement?	30	2,185
Make arrangements for initial disclosures?	71	2,252
Include discussion of discovery of electronically stored information?	40	2,232
In retrospect, help to develop a proportional discovery plan?	60	1,901

Table 7: If the Rule 26(f) meeting did not help you to better understand the opposing side's claims and defenses, why not? (Select all that apply.)

2012 ESOL Survey Response	(%)
I generally understood the opposing sides' claims and/or defenses prior to the meeting	77
At least one side was not cooperative in discussing claims and/or defenses	6
At least one side was not adequately prepared to discuss claims and/or defenses	6
Opponent raised no defenses beyond factual denials	6
Claims and defenses were not discussed	19
Other	6
N	1,153

Table 8: If the Rule 26(f) meeting did not increase the chances of a prompt resolution or settlement, why not? (Select all that apply.)

2012 ESOL Survey Response	(%)
At least one party was not interested in settlement or resolution at that point	60
At least one side was not adequately prepared to discuss settlement at that point	23
At least one party lacked sufficient information at that point	24
The sides were very close to reaching settlement prior to conference	3
Other	13
N	1,522

Table 9: If the Rule 26(f) meeting did not help in making arrangements for initial disclosures, why not? (Select all that apply.)

2012 ESOL Survey Response	(%)
At least one side was not adequately prepared to discuss initial disclosures	14
At least one side was not cooperative in discussing initial disclosures	11
The parties agreed to forego initial disclosures	8
The initial disclosure obligation was clear prior to the meeting	58
Other	15
N	645

Table 10: If the Rule 26(f) meeting did not, in retrospect, help to develop a proportional discovery plan, why not? (Select all that apply.)

2012 ESOL Survey Response	(%)
Discussion failed to adequately address major claims or defenses in the case	15
Discussion failed to adequately address the parties' discovery needs	18
Factors that could not be anticipated complicated discovery	16
The parties could not agree on proportionality	17
At least one party was not cooperative at the meeting	12
At least one party was not adequately prepared	10
At least one party engaged in abusive discovery practices	10
The court allowed disproportionate discovery despite objections	4
Other	33
N	766

Table 11: Of those reporting discussion of preservation obligations with respect to electronically stored information at the Rule 26(f) meeting, percentage indicating that the discussion helped to clarify at least one side's obligations.

2012 ESOL Survey Response	Yes (%)	*N*
Your client's obligations		
Producing parties only	60	78
Producing and requesting parties	60	256
All producing parties	60	334
Opposing side's obligations		
Requesting parties only	83	72
Producing and requesting parties	71	226
All requesting parties	74	298

Table 12: If the Rule 26(f) meeting did not clarify your client's preservation obligations with respect to electronically stored information, why not? (Select all that apply.)

2012 ESOL Survey Response	(%)
My client's preservation obligations were clear prior to the conference	89
Opposing counsel was not cooperative in discussing preservation obligations	4
Opposing counsel was not adequately prepared to discuss preservation obligations	7
Factors that could not have been anticipated	2
Other	5
N	134

Table 13: If the Rule 26(f) meeting did not clarify the opposing side's preservation obligations with respect to electronically stored information, why not? (Select all that apply.)

2012 ESOL Survey Response	(%)
My opponent's preservation obligations were clear prior to the conference	80
Opposing counsel was not cooperative in discussing preservation obligations	9
Opposing counsel was not adequately prepared to discuss preservation obligations	10
Factors that could not have been anticipated	4
Other	5
N	78

Table 14: Was there a Rule 16(b) conference, either in person or by telephone, with the judge in the named case?

Category of Respondent	Yes, in person (%)	Yes, by telephone (%)	No (%)	N
All respondents	31	19	50	3,150
Respondents reporting Rule 26(f) meeting	38	22	39	2,296

Table 15: Why wasn't there a Rule 16(b) conference in person or by telephone? (Select all that apply.)

2012 ESOL Survey Response	(%)
The case was resolved before the conference could take place	40
The Rule 16(b) conference was conducted by correspondence	12
Case was not required to have Rule 16(b) conference under local rule or judicial order	24
Other	24
N	1,492

Table 16: Did lead counsel participate in the Rule 16(b) conference?

2012 ESOL Survey Response	(%)
For both sides	84
For only one side	14
For neither side	1
N	1,553

13

Table 17: Was the Rule 16(b) conference conducted by a district judge or a magistrate judge?

2012 ESOL Survey Response	(%)
District judge	50
Magistrate judge	47
Other	3
N	1,505

Table 18: Did the judge engage in a substantive discussion of the sampled case at the Rule 16(b) conference?

2012 ESOL Survey Response	(%)
Yes	63
No	37
N	1,427

Table 19: How long did the Rule 16(b) conference last?

2012 ESOL Survey Response	(%)
Less than 10 minutes	23
10–30 minutes	57
30 minutes–1 hour	17
More than 1 hour	3
N	1,568

Table 20: Cross-tabulation of reported length of Rule 16(b) conference and whether judge engaged in a substantive discussion of the case (respondents answering "yes" or "no").

2012 ESOL Survey Response	Yes (%)
Less than 10 minutes	31
10–30 minutes	69
30 minutes–1 hour	82
More than 1 hour	89
N	1,417

Table 21: Did the judge engage in a discussion of the proportionality of discovery requests relative to stakes?

2012 ESOL Survey Response	(%)
Yes	24
No	76
N	1,346

Table 22: Did the judge limit discovery to make it more proportional?

2012 ESOL Survey Response	(%)
Yes	16
No	84
N	1,350

Table 23: Did the judge set cut-off or due dates for the following? (Select all that apply.)

2012 ESOL Survey Response	(%)
Fact discovery	79
Expert discovery	70
No cut-offs for discovery	11
Joinder of additional parties	59
Amended pleadings	65
Dispositive motions	69
Can't say	11
N	1,587

Table 24: After the Rule 16(b) conference, did the court enter a scheduling order?

2012 ESOL Survey Response	(%)
Yes	94
No	6
N	1,529

Table 25: Did the court adopt the parties' proposed discovery plan without modification, with minor modifications, or with major modifications? (Select the best option.)

2012 ESOL Survey Response	(%)
Without modification	39
With minor modification	57
With major modification	4
N	1,208

Table 26: How often did the court allow for modification of the schedule set in the scheduling order? (Select the best option.)

2012 ESOL Survey Response	(%)
Modified frequently	6
Modified occasionally	50
Not modified, but case settled before deadlines were reached	30
Not modified and deadlines were enforced	15
N	1,252

Table 27: Have your pleading practices changed since the Supreme Court's decisions in *Twombly* and *Iqbal*? (Limited to attorneys who reported that they typically represent plaintiffs or represent plaintiffs and defendants about equally, respondents answering "yes" or "no" only.)

2012 ESOL Survey Response	(%)
Yes	50
No	50
N	1,449

Table 28: How have your pleading practices changed since *Twombly* and *Iqbal*? (Select the best option.) (Limited to respondents answering that their pleading practices have changed.)

2012 ESOL Survey Response	(%)
More factual investigation prior to filing	28
More factual detail in complaints	92
Screen cases more carefully	25
Raise different types of claims	12
Other	6
N	724